Life Gives to the Giver

Musings on Wellness, Success,
Marketing and Being an Entrepreneur

By Joe Polish

ISBN-13: 978-1-7338532-6-2 Paperback

ISBN-13: 978-1-7338532-5-5 eBook

Table of Contents

INTRODUCTION

I'm Joe Polish and I want to help you.

Let me just dive right into why: While, of course, we all have struggles, my childhood was challenging. As a result, I internalized a great deal of shame and believed the world wasn't safe. I had absolutely no self-esteem. And the only way I could cope with how terrible I felt was to do drugs.

But this isn't a book about that. This is a book that compiles some of my strongest beliefs—those things that have helped me to become what some people consider the "world's best connector."

Still, I want you to know that I didn't just stumble across these truths. I learned them through trial and error. I learned them because, once I was in a new environment and away from all the people I used drugs with, I began to build a life.

But I still struggled with my career. I sold gym memberships and then worked at a mental hospital before starting a carpet cleaning business.

I was soon $30,000 in debt, trying to run a business that wasn't working.

One day, a friend from high school invited me on a jet skiing trip. Just like anyone who's $30,000 in debt would feel, I hesitated because I didn't have the money for things like that.

But when the friend mentioned that a wealthy real estate investor was also going to be there, I decided I'd go on this trip so I could ask the wealthy investor what business I should be in, since clearly carpet cleaning wasn't working out.

The man asked if there were people in my line of work that were making money.

I told him there were but that those people had all sorts of resources I didn't.

The man said, "If there are people who are successful in your business and you're not, the problem isn't your business—it's you."

What I needed to do, the man went on to explain, was learn fundamental business skills; otherwise I would just switch to another industry, spend between six months and two years learning the technical skills required and then end up repeating the same bad business habits that weren't working.

Develop business skills that work, the man told me, and you'll have control over your life. Otherwise, you'll be chasing opportunities.

That's when I realized that I was 100 percent responsible for my success—or lack thereof.

And so I devoted myself to understanding marketing. This meant learning, reading, listening, stopping things that weren't working and applying everything that I was learning to my business.

And that's when I realized that selling was all about getting someone intellectually and emotionally engaged and that marketing was all about storytelling (for a more thorough explanation of my feelings about selling, check out the transcript of my "Is Selling Evil?" video on the topic at the end of this book).

One of the first lessons I stumbled upon was Gary Halbert's advice to "can and clone yourself." So I hired a copywriter, using $1,800 I didn't have, to write something called "A Consumer's Guide to Carpet Cleaning." I started mailing that report out, along with special offers, and also set up a pre-recorded phone message that people were instructed to listen to before hiring a carpet cleaner. In a six-month period, I went from making $2,300 per month to $12,300. I ended up becoming a millionaire by the age of 30.

But success isn't just about money. My goal is to help create well-rounded entrepreneurs and that's why this book is divided into four sections:

1. Wellness

2. Success

3. Marketing

4. Entrepreneurship (with a special add-on at the end: the transcript of an interview I did that went viral called "Is Selling Evil?")

You really need all these things if you're going to be truly successful. You need to be well-rounded.

Creating well-rounded entrepreneurs is what I do with Genius Network and GeniusX, the two marketing groups I run.

They are the highest-level marketing groups in the entire world (Genius Network costs $25,000 per year to join while GeniusX costs $100,000) and almost all of the members are running multi-million-dollar companies.

My mission in life is to diminish human suffering. If any of the lessons I've compiled here diminishes yours, I've done my job. And I hope, by applying these ideas in your own business and life, I can help you do yours.

I also hope you'll connect with me on Facebook, download my podcasts and find out more about Genius Network.

And with that, I give you wisdom I've collected over the years on four crucial elements of life.

WELLNESS

Make More Money Getting Physical

You want to make more money?

Wake up every morning and meditate.

Do yoga.

Exercise.

Eat good, healthy food.

Be careful what you put into your body.

Get into a group with like-minded people. The beauty of getting together with a group is that it gives you perspective. When you are around people who have been there, done that, and can inspire you, it's great. There's power in proximity. As my good friend Tony Robbins says, "Proximity Is Power."

In order to actually get your body to do the things your brain is saying to do, remember: the issues are in the tissues. It's a PHYSICAL thing. You have to physically get your body aligned with your desires, your dreams, and your thoughts. If you want to effect change, put a physical practice into your life.

You can learn the greatest marketing strategies on the planet, but kicking things into gear has a lot to do with how you frame who you are and what you do. If you start thinking of yourself as an ATHLETE (not just a business owner), you will interact with yourself and the world on a different level.

No One Gives a Sh*t (and That's Great News)

The beauty of being your own boss is that you are your own boss. You can write and rewrite the rules whenever you want.

The worst thing about being your own boss is that you are your own boss. So, you want to create mechanisms to keep yourself accountable...

You want to start thinking: What is E.L.F.® – Easy, Lucrative and Fun – in your business and life?

When is the last time you had a Super Happy Fun Day?

When is the last time you had a date night with your partner?

When was the last time you called someone who was instrumental in helping you in your life and said, "Thank you. I love you. I want to send you a gift. I want to hang out with you…"

As my good friend Dan Sullivan says, "Entrepreneurs who are too tightly scheduled can't transform themselves."

As entrepreneurs, we need to constantly do so much to feel like we're valuable. Anyone, including myself, who puts themselves out there with podcasts, videos, books, and more wants the world to like them. We want the applause; we want the validation. This is great if it helps people, but if your whole world revolves around your ego, it's a very empty way to live.

You can make a lot of money and be very well known, but, again, it's a very empty way to live.

What will make you feel your best is completely up to you. No one gives a sh*t about your life the way you care about your life. Maybe your family cares. Maybe someone who is an amazing friend would take a bullet for you...

But if you think about it, what would you die for in this world?

WHO would you die for?

What's so important you would die for it? Are you giving those things the time, attention, and energy they deserve and need?

Or are you consumed by all the trivial nonsense that is constantly there?

Obligation Elimination

I like doing a lot of things, but I only like to commit to things that are E.L.F.® – Easy, Lucrative, and Fun.

I only like committing to things and people that align with me.

There are many distractions vying for your time and attention. The number one thing to protect, as it relates to how well you work, is your attention. And what takes up your attention is all the obligations.

People are too busy stepping over gold coins and picking up the bronze and silver coins. If you can identify the gold coins, and spend your time picking those up, it changes everything. And what is a gold coin for you will not be a gold coin for someone else. Everyone has different gold coins.

You have to focus on what the gold coins are FOR YOU and focus on what is E.L.F.® (Easy, Lucrative, and Fun) FOR YOU.

Be willing to destroy anything in your life that isn't excellent. There's plenty of time to do all the things you need to do to make a lot of money, have an awesome life, and have fun. But those things are being crowded out by all the stuff that isn't excellent.

Obligation Elimination. These two words can change everything for you…

A Simple Way to Make Work Work (and Make Your Life More E.L.F.®)

My friend Kathy Kolbe says, "The time to quit working is when working is no longer working."

If you are reading and you find that you have to read a sentence over and over, just stop. Go do something that doesn't require your brain to try to process, because it's no longer working.

If you're working on a relationship, or business things, and they're no longer working – quit them.

Arianna Huffington said something incredibly smart: "One of the best ways to complete a project is to drop it."

Some games in life, the only way you win is you don't play.

A lot of people wind up trying to get good at the stuff they're no good at. As my friend Dan Sullivan says, "If you spend your life strengthening your weaknesses, at the end of your life you will have a lot of strong weaknesses."

Do what you're really good at.

Do what you're aligned with.

Do what is E.L.F.® for you – Easy, Lucrative and Fun.

Look at your life and business as a game and set it up so you win. Have the best players. Have the best strategy. Have the best tools. And don't play games that aren't worth playing.

Nurturing Relationships

Which relationships do you want to nurture?

Whoever it is for you, it requires consistency. Like a farm, you need to take care of the soil. You need to tend to it. The same goes for relationships.

When I was in high school, I owned a pickup truck. I had several friends who only called me when they needed to move or needed to borrow my truck. They would ask me, "Can you come over and help me move my stuff?" And I would help them, and then I wouldn't hear from them for a while.

There are a lot of people who the only time you hear from them is when they need something.

Don't be one of those people. Determine who the top relationships are in your life, and then stay in touch with those people.

Holding onto Self-Destructive Behavior

There's a phrase used in recovery and 12-step programs: "Your best thinking got you here."

Imagine someone struggling with alcoholism or internet addiction or gambling or food or work-aholism or gaming, etc., and his or her life is just not working.

Maybe his life is in shambles.

Maybe her life is unmanageable from the perspective of being completely out of control, homeless, or even near death.

Maybe he or she is a functional addict running a business and married, but has a secret double-life.

In all these cases, their best thinking got them there.

Where you're currently at now is your current level of habits, biochemistry, diet, rituals and more. Good or bad, what you have done up to this point has gotten you to where you are now.

There is no human who is all good or all bad. We're all just humans.

We have flaws.

We have challenges.

We have areas in which we excel – and others where we simply operate with courage even though we're fearful.

Be a Good Human

I try to bring people together in Genius Network so everyone is a giver – not a taker. I try to remove takers out of my life as quickly as possible.

I believe life gives to the giver and takes from the taker.

I don't like people who are exploitative.

One way I pick my inner circle friends is by looking at how someone who is more powerful treats people who are less powerful.

Are they rude to servers in restaurants?

Do they say thank you when someone holds a door open for them?

Are they unreasonably mean to their team members?

Don't be a jerk.

Be a cool human being.

Your Psychological Safety

Great business owners…great connectors…great people…they create our world to be SAFE.

We are safer than we've ever been in human history…but we're not psychologically safe.

Terrorists didn't just hijack airplanes on September 11; they hijacked the American media. And this global fear has only gotten worse over the years.

Today we have better access to medical care than we used to. We have better living conditions and luxuries other countries have never experienced. But psychologically, it's a different story.

If you can keep yourself psychologically in check, everyone will feel safer with you. That is, if you can truly TRANSFORM those areas of your life. If you can do that, then the sky's the limit.

If you really want to be happy and help keep yourself in check, learn how to meditate. I couldn't do it for years. It wasn't until I was trained in Transcendental Meditation that I found I could finally meditate. Before that, I never gave it enough time to do it. I wanted everything to be instantaneous.

The same thing applies to growing and building your business and transforming YOUR personal life.

You have to do the work, and you have to do it in a reasonable time.

For example, if you have trouble sleeping and you solve that one big problem, a multitude of other things in your life would be indirectly solved.

Ask yourself: What is one problem that will solve 100 other problems?

There are many strategies you can learn that, if put into place in your business and life, will solve many other things. THOSE are the things to look for. It's your job to seek those things out. THOSE are the things that will help breed psychological safety.

Psychological Upgrade

Genius Network Member Benjamin Hardy talks about giving yourself a "Psychological Upgrade."

You can shift your thinking about the things you do if you ask yourself one thing:

Will this activity give me a Psychological Upgrade?

This doesn't mean spending money on expensive stuff for the sake of spending money. That can sometimes be stupid.

Psychological Upgrades can be attained in all areas of your life by putting yourself in the right environment.

For example, if you want to improve your tennis game, don't play with someone who is as good as or worse than you. Play with someone who is going to challenge you.

I'd rather be in a room with the smartest people in the world vs. being the smartest person in the room.

The big idea is this: You always want to keep ratcheting up things in your life.

Some Simple Ways to Live a Better Life

If you want to dramatically enhance your entrepreneurial effectiveness, improve your ability to run a better business and a better life...

...ramp up your physical fitness by 5%.

Get better sleep.

Deal with your trauma.

When I'm not getting things done effectively, it's because some area of my personal life that I'm not looking at is messed up.

If you're not sleeping well, you have about 20 or 30 problems in your life that exist because you're not sleeping well. If you solve that ONE problem, all the other problems will get solved.

Some people think, "I have to go to 100 seminars on how to better focus." Try going to five seminars. Try dropping out of some things. Don't read a book a week and then write a post about how you figured out how to "hack" the system. Instead, master two books that are REALLY good – and don't read the other 50 books.

Information is being poured on us like an avalanche. Marketing today is algorithms. What are you listening to? What are you paying attention to? What are you clicking on? Algorithms are serving up to your brain what your behavior is showing you are interested in.

People often want to intellectualize without dealing with the underlying trauma they are experiencing.

But if you want to get better in your life:

Go to bed early.

Don't consume things that numb you.

Don't eat crappy food.

Meditate.

Learn how to breathe.

Become a Fit Animal

In business, you are going to have to have some level of marketing stamina.

This is why, when you start out, eating healthy, getting enough sleep and exercising are more important than figuring out how to run a company.

You have to be a fit animal. The more fit you are, the more capable you are of doing well in the jungle.

If you wake up at 60%, and you're immediately putting sugar, bad food, or caffeine into your body, that percentage goes down significantly. This isn't a moral thing. It's a question of asking whether these activities "make the boat go faster." If you start your morning already tired, and you wake up at 60%... what things can you do to increase that percentage?

What will get you to 70% or 80%?

If you can set up the right conditions and get yourself to 90% or even 100% every morning, it can transform everything.

Get a blank sheet of paper. Draw a line down the middle. On the left-hand side, at the top, write "SETUP." On the right-hand side, at the top, write "CONDITIONS." In the right column write out the conditions you want in your life. Do you want a more successful business? Better clients? More money? A better relationship? More sleep? An environment you love? What does success look like for you? Then, on the left side, write the setup that needs to exist for those conditions to happen. What's the setup you need to make those conditions a reality?

To get the conditions you want, you need a certain type of setup. Put pencil to paper and start planning this out. Create the right setup. Become a fit animal.

Driving Lessons
for Entrepreneurs

Many entrepreneurs want to tap into something that will better direct them. But what do you do when your drive is driving you into walls or off cliffs?

What do you do when you feel squirrely?

Or lost?

Or just super anxious?

The alcoholic poet Charles Bukowski once said, "Take a writer away from his typewriter and all you have left is the sickness that started his writing in the first place." Not all entrepreneurs are sick, but this does relate to workaholism...

Anyone who is a growth minded person is driven and has a desire to grow. But what drives them to a state of overwhelm? Where they have no free time and the obsession with work prevents them from having any joyful personal time?

The psychologist Mihaly Csikszentmihalyi mentions how the same neural pathways that achievers, entrepreneurs, performers, etc. use to get into a flow state are the same neural pathways that an addict uses for self-destruction.

We're driving down the same road, but some people are crashing and killing themselves...and others are winning races.

Here's one solution: Give entrepreneurs better driving lessons.

Many people will never transform if they don't UNLEARN. Continuing to fill your head and life with data that is not helping you change is not the answer. Unlearning is more important than learning. Think about this for a while. Or maybe sit silently and stop taking your thoughts so seriously or thinking so hard. Lighten up, you will live longer and be happier if you do.

So many driven entrepreneurs are fighting addictions. They may not even call it an addiction, but they go to seminars, books, coaches, palm readers, etc. searching for a semblance of peace of mind, community and hope.

The difference, in many cases, is how you drive.

If you haven't done it lately or maybe ever before...go take a yoga class or get a massage. Go see a movie or a comedy show. And if it's really hard for you to just let go, ask: "What do I need to unlearn that is preventing me from having more fun, joy and relaxation in my life?"

When You're Overwhelmed...

When you're overwhelmed, think about everything on your plate as: POSSIBILITY, PROBABILITY, TIME and MONEY.

Here's how it works:

Dump all the projects and things on your mind onto a list. Then, for each item ask:

1. How POSSIBLE is it that this will work?

2. How PROBABLE is it that this will work?

3. How much TIME is this going to take?

4. How much MONEY will this actually make me?

The Importance of Adversity

Most change in life comes through adversity.

Most breakthroughs come out of having to break something.

To have a breakthrough, you have to break something.

If you look at times in your life where you had the greatest awareness or greatest shift, it's probable it came out of pain.

Maybe someone died who was close to you.

Maybe you had a breakup that felt like your heart had been ripped out of your chest.

Maybe you had another traumatic experience.

Most shifts come out of a painful area of life.

There are areas of life that work and areas of life that don't work. Most lessons and breakthroughs come out of an area of life that doesn't work and you're forced to face it, and make a change.

You won't go through this life without difficult things happening – but it's all fertilizer. It's all how you use it. There is plenty of fertilizer in the world to grow beautiful things – or – you can focus on how things suck and never grow. If you do the latter, you won't be able to make any breakthroughs because you're looking at it through a distorted lens. It's a choice.

Make the choice to grow.

The World of Social Media

The world of social media... There are many people who put more effort into getting "likes" than they do pursuing their own lives.

Almost every social media company hires attention engineers. Their entire job is to design their platform in a way that keeps people engaged so that they keep posting and chasing likes. Most people are oblivious to how compulsive their behavior is as a result of this conditioning. Social algorithms understand your behavior better than you do.

Marketing today is algorithms. People are designing very smart systems these days that will enslave you if you aren't paying attention.

If you don't manage modern life, it will manage you.

Social media can be utilized in many ways. You can reach lots of people with your message through technology that wasn't available before. So, there are great things that come with social media and technology, but there is a dark side to everything. There is no perfect system that is 'all good' with no disadvantages.

Most people don't use technology; technology uses them.

Most people don't use social media; they are used by it.

Most people don't own the things they own; the stuff owns them.

The goal is to increase your consciousness and positive, healthy rituals. If you internally take care of yourself, you won't feel like your self-worth and self-esteem equates to the number of likes or followers you have.

That Which You Fear Controls You

I was very disconnected growing up. I was shy. I was introverted. I didn't feel comfortable talking to people…

The journey of recovery, and the pursuit of becoming more connected, was my saving grace.

People want to be connected. No one wants to be disconnected. If someone feels disconnected, they may lean on artificial means of trying to connect.

When people interact, they are either in communication, or they are trying to escape. A great example is when you are at an event or in public and someone comes up to talk with you. You might feel an immediate affinity with that person... or, you could feel like something is off. It's worth thinking about why that is.

What is your vibe? What is the energy you're giving off that allows people to connect?

I started connecting with others when I realized that if I didn't, I wouldn't get what I wanted out of life. I couldn't get things like friendships, opportunities, business, money, etc., if I didn't learn to connect. So, I started putting myself out there.

It's one thing to be shy and introverted. It's another to be isolated and incapable of interacting with other people.

That which you fear controls you; that which you fear and face, you can control it. Overcoming certain fears and challenges is the way to grow.

Habits

I don't believe in "good" habits or "bad" habits. I believe in habits.

If you wake up every day and yell at your spouse, kick the dog, smoke five cigarettes, guzzle two cups of coffee, and eat an Egg McMuffin... you don't have a bad habit. You've simply developed a habit of waking up, yelling at your spouse, drinking coffee, smoking cigarettes, and eating crappy food.

It boils down to certain actions done in a certain way produce a certain result. There are success habits that will produce a great result.

What are the habits you can put in place that will serve you? What is the one habit that will move your life in the direction you want? Write it down and start developing it every day until you have mastered that habit.

Addiction is a Solution

Letting go of who you've been for who you can become is a process of letting go. It's a process of eliminating the current solution you're using to try and soothe yourself.

As my friend Dr. Gabor Maté says, "The question is not why the addiction, but why the pain."

When we see addictions, we are seeing someone in pain... someone in fear... someone feeling loneliness, depression, anger, isolation, and more. The addiction happens to be the way they are scratching the itch.

Think of the pain metaphorically as the itch. There's nothing wrong with wanting pain to go away; it's the method you use to scratch the itch.

It's also worth pointing out that when I look at people who have addictions, many have a lot of physical pain. It's possible that the same manifestations that cause addiction... (or cause someone to self-destruct... or to try and get the dopamine hits they are looking for through behaviors or chemicals... or cause repressed emotions and a feeling of not being okay in the world...) are the same things that manifest as physical pain.

In this way, the pain is a way for our body to try and protect itself from feeling feelings it does not want to feel.

People who look at addicts as moral degenerates need to understand

something...

There's not a person on the planet that has some unmanageable, out of control behavior who WANTS that.

When we hold onto any self-destructive behavior, we do it because it is serving us in some way.

Some people may say, "They DO want it, because they are obviously doing it." But the truth is, the pain serves them to the degree that it helps them scratch the itch.

In this way, addiction IS a solution for people; it's just not a good one.

It's one that could kill them.

Your Health

There is a proverb that says, "Those who have their health have 1,000 dreams; those who do not have health have only one."

If you have your health, you also have space for dreams and aspirations.

Don't lose your health. People who lose it are willing to give anything – money, relationships, everything – to get it back.

So, don't squander it.

Take care of your health.

You Are a Million Dollar Racehorse

I interviewed an individual years ago named Terri Lonier, who wrote a book called Working Solo. During the interview, we talked about "The Million Dollar Racehorse."

Think of yourself as a Million Dollar Racehorse…

If you owned a Million Dollar Racehorse, how would you treat it?

You wouldn't shove fast food down its throat.

You wouldn't cause it to have sleep deprivation.

You would make sure it gets the best trainers, the best tracks, and the best everything.

You would take care of that Million Dollar Racehorse, because it needs to win races to make you money.

So, YOU are that Million Dollar Racehorse. If you treat yourself any other way, you are likely messing yourself up.

Part of this is about how you physically take care of yourself. It also involves who you hang out with. Cut all ties with dishonest, lazy people.

Look at the environment in which you work. Look at the clients you have. Which ones are E.L.F.® – Easy, Lucrative, and Fun?

Everything I attempt to do is that which is E.L.F.®

Take a look at your business and life and ask:

Is your environment E.L.F.?

Are the people you associate with E.L.F.?

Are you treating yourself in a way that makes your life and business more E.L.F.?

Make your life and business E.L.F. and treat yourself like the Million Dollar Racehorse you are.

SUCCESS

There's Money in Context

One of the greatest books in my opinion is *What to Expect When You're Expecting*.

Every day there are a slew of new expecting mothers. Someone is getting pregnant every day. Everyday someone wants to get pregnant. And so on.

Every year, they just update the material, put in new links, and that book will just stay on the best seller list for as long as it's relevant -- and -- it's the go-to book. Oftentimes, if you're just a great organizer of stuff, you can make a lot of money. There's a lot of money in context. Not necessarily content. Giving people a better way to think about something.

Right now, you can think of certain conditions.

People don't buy products and services; they buy conditions. They're buying events. They're buying context.

The Best Way to Read a Book: Get Dirty

I remember Eben Pagan mentioned a great way to get the most out of reading.

He didn't say this to be sexist, but he basically said, "Your book is your bitch."

A lot of people read books cover to cover, even when they aren't into the book and they aren't finding it as useful as they thought it would be.

They have this guilt they put on themselves about "finishing the book."

You may even pick up a book recommended by someone and you get 20 minutes into it completely unimpressed. Yet, you keep reading it.

Stop that.

If you don't immediately resonate with something, forget it. You don't need to read the whole thing.

Take what's useful, leave the rest.

And don't be afraid to get the book dirty. Write in it. Highlight what's important to you. Jot stuff down in the margins. Circle what pops out. Rip pages out.

This way, when you look at your notes, the important points stand out.

The same logic applies to ebooks and whatever else you read on your tablet, Kindle, iPad, Smart Phone, whatever.

Mark it up, make notes and highlight it. Just don't write on your computer with a big marker because that would be pretty idiotic.

The Five-Part Formula for a Super Successful Event

When you're doing events, several things help.

These aren't always necessary, but if you can get all five, your chances for success and happy attendees are much higher.

1) You need Shamu The Whale. People go to Sea-World because they want to see Shamu. So, you need a Shamu. (Also known as a "well known person.")

2) You need a great location.

3) You need great food.

4) You need great discussions.

5) You need great people.

Put these five ingredients together, and any event you put on will have a much higher chance of success as long as you market it effectively.

Most people don't market events successfully and they think it's really easy.

It's not. I've been doing events successfully for almost 20 years.

I can assure you it's a heck of a lot easier if you utilize great marketing and my five-part formula.

You Don't Need Social Media to be Successful

I was born in 1968.

My age range is the only generation that went from black and white to colored televisions; to cordless telephones; to pagers; to fax machines; to computers; to the internet; to mobile phones and smart phones.

Throw some social media into the mix and wear a pair of Google Glasses and things get interesting.

As I write this, 3D printing is becoming a very big deal and it will change the world of business in ways people can't even imagine, along with AI (Artificial Intelligence), crowdfunding, even cryonics.

Yep, interesting things ahead.

Now people born today will never be in an age where they are not totally electronically connected.

This has all happened in about a 20-year period.

What we're going to see happen in the next five years is going to be mind boggling. Especially when, as my friend Peter Diamandis says, three billion new people come online.

It's fascinating how many people are connected.

But what you don't need is thousands or millions of friends online in order to be profitable and successful.

That's silly and too complicated for most people.

What you need is enough people to think what you're doing is awesome, will speak to it, will be advocates for it, will edify it, and will buy it.

How Much You Get Out of an Event

How much you get out of any event has a lot to do with what you do AFTER the event is over.

As my friend Eben Pagan says, SPEED OF IMPLEMENTATION is the secret. THAT is what determines whether the idea will take hold. Ideas, aspirations and ambitions have a shelf life without action. The more you can ENGAGE with those ideas and elements, and do something with them, the better.

After you've reviewed everything you got from an event, ask yourself:

What are the Elegant Ideas?

What's the one thing that solves 100 problems?

What are the ideas that, if I actually implemented them in my life and business, would produce a GREAT RESULT? Then, take it seriously and take action.

BTW - there will also be things you will have learned that are great ideas – but they aren't great ideas right now. So, you want to also have a NOT NOW LIST (a safe place to put those great ideas you don't want to lose).

How to Live a High Integrity Life

Here are five truths for living a high integrity life:

1. If you want more selection in your life, be more selective.

2. Have standards for how you operate. If you lie down with dogs, you wake up with fleas.

3. There's no such thing as a good business deal with a bad partner. Align with people who align with you.

4. As my friend Betty Rocker posted: "Sometimes the grass is greener on the other side because it's fake."

5. Don't try to adopt someone else's value system. Adopt your own value system and live into it. Real human happiness doesn't come from consuming others' values, but by producing your own.

Struggle, Opportunity and Goals

Here are three thoughts about…

Struggle:

Many successful people have figured out how to take silent battles and pain, and transform them into productivity. Most people cannot, and don't, do this. The vast majority of people do not read books. The vast majority of people do not go to seminars. The vast majority of people do not seek out self-improvement.

If there is a commonality among successful people – it's struggle. And, it's being able to overcome the struggle and tap into resource-fulness that makes one successful.

Opportunity:

Successful people take intelligent risks while seeking out recipes and solutions for success. They put themselves in front of opportunity. Opportunity is always there; the question is whether you are availing yourself of it.

Goals:

Goals are dreams that are taken seriously. A lot of people have dreams, but they don't take them very seriously. The people that do, have goals. When you attach action to those goals, you produce results.

Focus on Your Strengths

What if you started focusing on your strengths instead of your weaknesses?

As Dan Sullivan says, "If you spend too much time working on your weaknesses, all you end up with is a lot of strong weaknesses."

Most of the things people are really good at, they feel guilty about doing. They tend to put a lot of time and effort into things they suck at or that they think they have to do. The things they are good at seem to be so effortless and "too easy."

Productivity is maximum results for the least amount of time. Leverage is maximum results for the least amount of effort. Focusing on your strengths makes you productive and gives you leverage.

What are your strengths? What are your amazing skills and capabilities? Where is your performance excellent?

Develop those things and think of it as marketing.

Bring Clarity
to the Confusion

Here's something to remember about becoming more influential and persuasive:

Someone who can show up and bring clarity to the confusion of someone else's situation has the opportunity to do something great.

As my friend Richard Rossi says, "Wherever there is anxiety, there's opportunity."

If you look for a person's anxieties and ease or eliminate that pain for them, then you have a magic moment.

You can get people to do all kinds of things for YOU by doing things for THEM.

Some people think they have to manipulate people or use people like puppets to get what they want.

But what if you simply showed up and were really useful?

This will make you both feel good.

Make Yourself Useful

I believe that all human beings have some area of their life that causes them a lot of pain. It also causes them to fight silent battles.

They build their businesses and their image, but there is this thing inside them that HURTS.

What people don't realize about a lot of really successful and wealthy people is that a lot of their success is driven by this pain and angst. No one really feels sorry for the rich guy or gal with a beautiful house on the beach – but if you got to know them and saw some of the ghosts from their past, you might think differently about their lives.

There is so much jealousy and envy that exists in the world. Realizing that every person has a certain level of consciousness that allows them to do what it is they do, makes it easier to build rapport with them.

Think about this: How do you help someone if you resent them? How do you help YOURSELF if you resent YOURSELF? How well do you do with something if you're disconnected from it? The answer: not well.

Instead, you can start to think about how to make your life and business help better people's lives. You can get paid well for this. People will appreciate you for this. People will refer you to others when you do this.

The more you can make yourself useful, the more you will meet and build relationships with a lot more people. And this doesn't apply only to business. It applies to parenting, dating, and every other aspect of life.

How will YOU help people become better? What will YOU do to make yourself more useful?

Bet on the Jockey

People have a good idea of where their mindset will allow them to go.

Some people break out of that mindset. But for the most part, people stay within their cliques and comfort zones.

Ten years from now, most people will be 10-years-older versions of who they are today.

The few who transcend this tendency have a unique quality inside them.

It's not access to knowledge. (If you take driven people and give them minimal knowledge, they will figure out how to make things work.)

It's not the information.

It's not the seminar.

It's not the group.

It's the person.

If you're going to bet on the jockey or the horse, I would bet on the jockey. Because a smart jockey will get off the wrong horse.

Nine Valuable Lessons

Here are nine valuable lessons I've learned in business:

1. You will often spend more money to get clients than you make in immediate profits. The real money isn't made on the front end -- it's made on the backend.

2. Marketing is your OFFER, the LIST, and COPY. You want to make the right offer to the right list with compelling copy.

3. Using premiums and incentives will increase the value of your offers.

4. In business, you need four things: Marketing, Management, Margins, and the right Model.

5. Focus on getting the right clients, at the right price, in a more efficient and effective way. Then automate the process.

6. Make sure your marketing is E.L.F® Marketing – Easy, Lucrative, and Fun.

7. Have a product or service that is so good you will be proud to have it owned by the people you love and care about.

8. Then, put as much marketing muscle behind that product or service as you can.

9. Have a beginner's mind. Don't be too cool for school.

Implement Stick Strategies

Many people operate in a very shallow, superficial way. And I can empathize with why that is.

Many people are ADD and distractible. They are looking for the magic pill.

They are hoping that "this one" is going to be "the thing."

People get caught up in novelty, newness, and promiscuity.

In business, being nice, caring, or the most connecting sometimes isn't enough to keep people around.

So what should you do?

Implement STICK STRATEGIES.

How are you making what you do so invaluable that people won't want to leave?

Value Creation

Dan Sullivan developed a concept called the "Value Creation Monopoly."

Here's what it means: Imagine there is an electric company that is a monopoly. If they are the only electric company in town, they don't have to pick up the phone. They don't have to get to your house right away. They can treat you poorly. Why? Because there are no competitors. As a monopoly, they can control things. Yet, the moment there's competition, they have to step up their game.

What YOU want is to have a Value Creation Monopoly. This is when people give you business because you've created SO much value for them, not because they have no other choice. There are people you do business with simply because they are really good people and you WANT to give them business.

I like giving business to people I like.

I like giving business to people I care about.

In fact, I'll continue cutting checks to people even if I'm not currently fully using their services because I never forget the value I've received in the past. To me, it's just a way of being. I wish more people operated like this, and I hope that you do.

Deliver Good News
to Yourself

We are a country of chemistry. People are constantly in pain. This is why you see so much garbage sold.

If you're presenting something that is actually going to help people, you are transforming people's bad news into good news. In fact, most of the money you're going to make in your life is not from good news; it's from bad news…

If you break your ankle, that's bad news; if you're a doctor, that's good news.

If you're hungry, that's bad news; if there's a restaurant, that's good news.

Imagine if there weren't products and services to help people deal with all the bad news. You are dealing with bad news all the time. Most of your money is going to come from transforming other people's bad news into good news.

The way to get better at this is to take the things in your head and turn them into more good news.

Be a merchant of delivering good news to yourself.

When you start responding to life instead of reacting, things start to change. Your revenue goes up. Your mood gets better. Your ability to manage and repel people who are not good for you gets better.

Freedom = Having An E.L.F. (Easy, Lucrative, and Fun) Business

How do you know when you're being successful?

What does success look like for you?

Is it more money? Is it spending more time away from your business?

When we look at the entrepreneurial playing field, there are three types of people. The first person is what we might think of as unsuccessful. The second person is what we traditionally think of as successful. And here's something interesting: these first two people are actually more alike than they are different. The truth is, traditionally successful people can have almost the same kind of business unsuccessful people have...

A H.A.L.F. Business™.

This type of business is Hard, Annoying, Lame, and Frustrating - H.A.L.F.™. A traditionally successful person may actually have a Hard, Annoying, LUCRATIVE, and Frustrating business - but it's still H.A.L.F.™.

Yet, there's a third type of entrepreneur. This third type of entrepreneur is TRULY successful - by all measures. They have what's called an E.L.F. Business®. An E.L.F. Business is one that is Easy, Lucrative, and Fun. When you have this type of business, you really start to have more of what my friend Dan Sullivan, founder of Strategic Coach, calls The Four Entrepreneurial Freedoms: Time, Money, Relationship, and Purpose.

So here's the question: What stops us?

One thing: Barriers.

Imagine a giant wall separating two worlds: The H.A.L.F.™ world, and the E.L.F.® world. The reality is the wall that separates these two worlds is mostly psychological. Some of these psychological barriers might show up as...

* "I want to make more money but I don't know how"

* "I work 80 hours a week and I don't know how to work less"

* "I don't have any free time or do anything fun anymore because I'm a slave to my business" and so on...

We all have psychological barriers, and if we become more aware of the barriers between these worlds, we become better at eliminating them and developing the skills, habits, and capabilities that bring us into (and keep us in) the E.L.F.® world.

Now, what can you do today to start getting into the E.L.F.® world? Here's an action step: begin where you are, and utilize the resources you have. Start thinking through all the things in your life that are available to you and focus on those things that are most important. Once you identify what is most important, you can start working through the barriers between you and your E.L.F. Business®.

Anthony Greenback wrote a book called *The Book of Survival*. In that book, he says, "To live through an impossible situation, you don't need to have the reflexes of a Grand Prix driver, the muscles of a Hercules, the mind of an Einstein. You simply need to know what to do."

I've known incredibly intelligent people that have failure after failure, and I've known people who haven't even graduated high school who have built multi-million dollar businesses. The difference that makes the difference is learning and developing the skills, habits, and capabilities that take you from a H.A.L.F.™ life to an E.L.F.® life.

Take Action

There are three ways you can learn something:

1. You can learn through the school of hard knocks.

2. You can learn through the experience of others.

3. You can learn by teaching and sharing with other people.

One of the reasons I love doing podcasts – The Genius Network podcast (GeniusNetwork.com); I Love Marketing podcast (iLoveMarketing.com); 10X Talk podcast (www.10XTalk.com) – is because they are a great vehicle to not only distribute great ideas out into the world, but also they accelerate my education and learning.

And if you want to know a secret to making your learning pay off, it's something my friend Eben Pagan talks about…

Speed of Implementation.

The moment you hear or learn something, if you can identify the first step that will move you towards taking that idea, concept, method and/or strategy and putting it into action, you will be much closer to producing results. The problem many people face is they sit on things. Yet, as the late, great copywriter

Gary Halbert used to say, "You will accomplish more through movement than you ever will through meditation."

How to Deal with Fear

A question I've been asked is "How do I deal with fear?"

Whether you are trying to start something new or get to the next level, many people try to "overcome" or "conquer" fear. To a certain degree, that may work for a period of time.

However, the question is really: How do you ride the fear?

When I first started out in business in my early 20's, I never had it in my mind that I would ever speak in front of people. I was an incredibly shy and introverted kid. I had trouble speaking with people one-on-one, let alone speaking in front of an audience. I had incredible insecurity around that.

I started reading self-improvement books, and there was a line from one of them that suggested that whatever you fear and don't face will control you; whatever you fear and take steps to face, you will control it – or at least you will get better at how you interact with it.

I used to try to power my way through certain fears. Eventually, I got to a point where I simply tried to dance with the fear. I learned how to get into flow with it.

Since the fear is always there, treat it like riding a wave. Remember: Anything worth doing is worth doing poorly, in the beginning. Now, granted, if you suck at it, and you practice, and you still suck at it, and you practice, and you're no good at it, and it doesn't energize you – sometimes the best way to get out of a hole is to quit digging. There are certain times when giving up is actually smart. Instead, put your attention and energy on those things that produce for you. Take your talents and develop them to where you get really good, and ride the wave of fear.

Another line I heard was to do something every day that scares you. Now, of course, context is important here. Don't go run out in front of traffic, obviously. Simply take certain levels of challenges that force you to grow. If you do that, you build your confidence muscles.

All of this requires courage. Courage never feels good. Courage is never comfortable. When my friend and founder of Strategic Coach, Dan Sullivan, was in the army, his sergeant taught him a valuable lesson about fear. His sergeant said, "Fear is wetting your pants. Courage is doing what you're supposed to do with wet pants."

There is opportunity in your anxiety. The things that cause you the most fear, the things that cause you the most pain, the things that seem insurmountable … those are the things that might have within them the highest likelihood of your future progress.

Are You Enjoying Your Profit?

Profit is only useful to the degree that you can use it.

You can have a super profitable business, but if you don't have any time to enjoy your profits, what's the point?

Yet this is where most entrepreneurs are at. Most people who create the most stuff in the world are actually the ones who benefit the least...

Someone who is running a spa is oftentimes the most stressed-out person from trying to direct their business.

You want to get to the point where you are able to enjoy what you put out there in the world.

You want to be able to enjoy your profits. You want to make everything more E.L.F.® – Easy, Lucrative, and Fun.

What's Your Opportunity Filter?

Dan Sullivan, the founder of Strategic Coach, has a great thinking process called "The Opportunity Filter." It lays out the five ways you get paid in business and in life.

You can get paid with money – but you can also get paid when people appreciate you, utilize you, refer you, or it enhances you.

Early on in my entrepreneurial life, I used to read books emphasizing how much your time is worth per hour. I would always find myself spending time with people and on things that didn't make the most money – and I would beat myself up because of it. I'd question why I was spending time on these things and people that didn't bring as high of a financial return as if I had put that focus on something else. But, once I learned Dan Sullivan's model, I realized it wasn't JUST about being rewarded with money.

For example, for me, my criteria of getting paid is as follows: 1. Does it enhance me? 2. Are they utilizing me? 3. Do they appreciate me? 4. Do they refer me? 5. Does it pay me money?

So, monetary payoff is actually fifth on the list for me. Money has to be there, but it's the fifth criteria.

If all you're getting for something is money – and you're not getting enhancement, appreciation, utilization and/or referrals – it's prostitution. A lot of people are engaged in prostitution, and they don't know it. If you're doing something simply for money and you're okay with that – great. But I like looking at other criteria as well.

How do YOU get paid? What's YOUR criteria?

I hope this helps you realize there are many ways to get rewarded, and money is just one of them.

People That Say Money Can't Buy Happiness...

Not all money is created equal. I like looking at things that are E.L.F.® Money: Easy, Lucrative and Fun.

People say that money can't buy happiness. But it can. I buy happiness all the time with money. If you use money to do things you like, such as eating at amazing restaurants, or travelling to cool places, or buying a material item that fills you with joy – you just bought yourself some happiness.

Yes, money won't solve a lot of things. Like Jim Rohn says, "You can't hire someone else to do your push-ups for you." And, yes, money can even make you miserable depending on how you experience it.

BUT...the pursuit of E.L.F.® Money is the best way to enhance your life.

I like to think of money as FUN TICKETS.

On top of this, people that say money can't buy happiness haven't given enough of it away. If you're able to give money or contribute to things that help other people and it makes them happy, you're able to buy some happiness for them.

And for people that still think money can't buy happiness -- well, I at least know poverty can't buy sh*t!

Assembling Unicorns

Genius Network member Jason Fladlien gave me some language around what I do…

I assemble unicorns.

I go out and find unicorns, and I put them together with each other.

Unicorns together change the world. (And unicorns in isolation, surrounded by donkeys, hate life.)

Really high level entrepreneurs need to find other high level people. So, I build a tribe of tribal leaders. That's what Genius Network is.

I do it by never asking anyone to do anything for me before creating value for them first. I also follow the philosophy of being nice to the people you meet on the way up; they are the same people you meet on the way down. (And if you want to know how to meet and establish relationships effectively with high level people, go listen to Episode #29 on I Love Marketing about The Magic Rapport Formula: https://ilovemarketing.com/episode-029-the-one-about-the-magic-rapport-formula/)

I'm just do my best to be valuable and useful.

So, here's the question:

How can YOU be more valuable?

How can YOU be more useful?

How can YOU assemble unicorns?

Where can you go to find an already existing stable of unicorns?

Getting Paid for the Result You Deliver

When I was selling to carpet cleaners, I delivered my material in the form of speeches, phone calls, videos and audios, strategies and more. There are many ways to deliver advice, motivation, inspiration, elegant insights and implementable ideas.

But what I was selling was how to make money. I was selling money at a discount. I would teach people how to double their business in six months or less. I would teach people how to get more clients. And what all this translated into as far as results are concerned, if they applied what I shared with them, was worth A LOT to them and ended up costing them nothing. What I do today is I sell money at a discount and I help build a better entrepreneur.

I made my mark with marketing, but now I make my mark with marketing being one of the hooks or triggers that connects people with other people. I now get paid to curate capabilities and wisdom and I have a system that connects individuals with each other and to business strategies, friendships, and more.

For example, in Genius Network, Joel Weldon is one person who has capabilities everyone can benefit from – even if they aren't a speaker. Jason Fladlien is another member who has webinar capabilities that are extremely valuable. Ben Hardy has writing capabilities that benefit Genius Network.

In YOUR world, what is the RESULT you deliver? How can you get paid for that RESULT, and not just for what you do?

"I've Heard That Before!"

Successful people are those who take action.

The sad part? Most people don't.

Speed of implementation and execution is really important.

There are a lot of good ideas out there...but they are useless if you don't use them.

I love the quote: "You ask for a new idea when you haven't used the first one I gave you."

Whenever a new idea is given, I hear people say, "I've heard that before!"

Then I ask them, "Oh, well, have you implemented it?"

They say, "Um, no."

Why are some people so insistent on getting a new idea they aren't going to use?

Don't be one of those people.

Be successful.

The Real Pricing Formula

How much you charge for something is based on your ability to sell it.

The better you get at selling something, the more you charge, and that's important to understand.

The reality about pricing formulas is this...

There is no better pricing formula other than how effective you are at selling.

Unless you're selling commodities, price is elastic.

I remember a story about one of the most successful salesmen (from the 1970's) for Nightingale-Conant, one of the top companies that sells personal development material.

This salesman would look for businesses and people that had bookshelves filled with books and audio tapes. Why? Because if they already showed some sign of buying this stuff, he would know he had a buyer. If they didn't have any books, he'd ask them, "How often do you read business books?" ...and if the person didn't read and buy them often, he wouldn't waste his time. He focused his efforts on people that already consumed.

Find people that are already participating, and get good at selling.

Results Only

On www.ILoveMarketing.com, Dean Jackson and I had a conversation where we asked these questions:

If you only got paid when you produced a result, how would you sell your stuff?

How would you communicate about your stuff?

How would you package your stuff?

Even if you never have to do it, going through the thinking process will completely change the way you talk about it, create it and offer it.

It will change the way you engage with your clientele.

Entrepreneurial Calluses

Trying to be an entrepreneur, and wearing all sorts of hats, is a tough gig.

When I started in my first real business (carpet cleaning in 1990), I was doing everything.

Accounting, list management, cleaning the carpets, answering the phone ...all of it.

And you know what you realize over time?

It's not that business gets easier. The BS is still there. But your tolerance level changes and hopefully your capabilities improve if you focus on always bettering yourself.

I think a lot of business success is simply having a high tolerance for crap.

Stuff that used to bother you just rolls off you as you become more successful.

The more you can accelerate that, the better.

The First Sale

The first person you have to sell is yourself.

The number one sales job you have to do every day is the sales job you do on yourself.

Why is what you're doing important?

What difference will it make?

What is the ideal outcome?

Dan Sullivan has a thinking tool called The Impact Filter.

I suggest you go to www.StrategicCoach.com and find out more.

Because when you wake up every day...

When you interact with the world...

When you're running your business...

When you're engaging people...

How well you do these things is related to how engaged and sold you are with yourself and what you're doing.

The Best Piece of Advice I Ever Got

I've interviewed Sir Richard Branson on business probably more times than anyone else. I'm also the largest individual fundraiser to Virgin Unite, Richard's charity.

And I remember being in Richard's kitchen on his island, Necker Island, a couple of trips ago. (My company does trips to Necker Island every year. $40,000 a person.)

So, as I was standing there, I asked Richard, "When's the last time you went to a grocery store?"

He looks at me and says, "I don't think I've ever been to the grocery store."

I said, "What do you mean? How is it possible you've never gone to a grocery store?"

So I followed up with, "Well, when's the last time you did laundry?" And Richard said, "I've never done laundry."

Perplexed, I said, "What do you mean you've never done laundry? What about when you were a kid?"

"My mum did my laundry," Richard said.

Then Richard simply said, "Joe, you hire people to do that stuff."

Then he said, "Taking the time to hire the right person will save you thousands of hours in the future in your life."

That was probably the best piece of advice I ever heard Richard say.

Think of all the hours you spend on stuff that if you just had someone else do that stuff...

And this doesn't just go for stuff you don't want to do, but also stuff they could do more effectively.

You Get in Life What You Negotiate

Some people consider other people lucky in business.

But the truth is, oftentimes, their luck is a result of them having marketing stamina.

They are willing to play the long game.

They maintain a positive attitude.

They fill their head with useful, enthusiastic ideas and insights, and they take them seriously.

As my good friend Dave Kekich, who has been paralyzed from the chest down in a wheelchair for half his life, says, "Enthusiasm covers many deficiencies."

When you are first starting out, you want to be as enthusiastic as possible because if you come across as needy, desperate, or show your backstage frustration or fear, it doesn't help.

I know many people who get up and give motivational talks who have had their head cradled in their hands at their desk or bed with tears rolling down their cheeks because they can't figure out how to get anyone to pay them. I can understand living in that fear. But the fact is, you can let that happen backstage when you're trying to figure it all out...but your front stage experience needs to be totally different. You need to suit up, be a pro and put your big boy or big girl pants on when you go out into the business world, and keep at it.

We've all had to do this. As a carpet cleaner, not only was I broke, I was also living off credit cards trying to figure out how to make it work. I learned marketing never thinking I would ever want to do marketing. To this day I wish I didn't have to do marketing. I do it because I don't live in a fantasy land.

This isn't "build it and they will come."

This isn't about just being a nice person and the world will beat a path to your door.

That isn't reality...and you know it.

So even if you fight and resist this, deep down inside you know you don't get in life what you deserve... you get in life what you negotiate.

You don't get in life what's fair, you get in life what you negotiate.

The money fairy isn't going to show up and just bestow money onto you. You have to go out and make yourself attractive and set up the conditions for people to find you.

If life was so wonderful and easy and being a nice, kind, caring person made people rich, everyone would be doing it. But the fact of the matter is, this is not a game for amateurs. If you treat it like an amateur sport, you will continue to play amateur sports. If you want to be a pro, ask: What do the pros read? What do the pros do? How do the pros develop themselves? And what do I need to do to be more of a pro?

MARKETING

What Needs Solved?

Many people struggle in their business because they haven't solved one problem.

What is one problem that, if solved, would solve 100 other problems?

A lot of times, that one problem is MARKETING.

Think about this: There are a lot of fish out there. Other people are in the same business as you. But they might be doing well, and you may not be. The questions to ask are: What are they fishing with? Where are they fishing? What are they doing differently?

You're one SALES LETTER or OFFER away from getting people to respond to you.

So ask yourself, "What Needs Solved?"

And remember: Don't waste time with people who are dispensing advice on how to do things that they themselves have not done. Hang around with winners, because winners find ways to win – and losers find ways to lose.

"I Don't Know How to Write" OR "I Don't Like Writing"

If you don't know how to write, or you don't like writing, but you have to...

Whether for content or to make offers or simply to sell...

Then record yourself talking it out. Record yourself doing a pitch for what you sell.

Just get your iPhone or a mini-recorder, and record yourself.

Then, just get it transcribed.

That becomes the basis of your writing.

You can do this for your sales letter, your articles, your book, and on and on.

And as soon as you have enough revenue, hire a copywriter.

A great copywriter could be worth millions to you.

You Can Make Money from Phone Books

You can make money from phone books. Really.

How?

Picture this: people pay money for display ads in phone books, even to this day.

Now, let's just imagine for a moment that you're a financial advisor and you specialize in helping dentists get their financial house in order.

You can go to the phone book, pull out all the dental ads, and make copies of them. Then, you find out what those dentists are paying for their ads. Say they are paying $500 a month for a half-page ad in your local phone book.

You then get the dentist's name and mailing address, and you put a letter in a FedEx envelope that says the following…

"Dear Bob,

I've attached a copy of your Yellow Pages ad to the top of this letter.

I've done this for a couple of reasons:

1. You're currently paying $500/month for this ad. Therefore, you're trying to generate business.

2. Making money is not the same thing as managing money. So, I've got a couple of things I could share with you.

I happen to know a lot about marketing, because, as you can see, I actually know how much you paid for your ad – and I'm sending you this Direct Mail piece to tell you about it. And, I specialize in helping dentists with their financials.

In fact, here are some comments from other dentists like you…"

It's the same idea behind any service offering, but in this case, you're adding in some extra things…like the fact that everyone is going to read a letter WITH THEIR AD ATTACHED TO IT! (This is called a grabber. It's a way to get people's attention).

Also, you've already emotionally hooked them because you've identified how much they are spending trying to generate business.

You can then go on to include a number for them to call you, and even if they decide (or you decide) it isn't a right fit to work with you, you still send them one of the most effective marketing books that has helped your clients generate two to three times more business in their dental practice (a.k.a. Your Book!)

All of this is designed to help you think in ways to become a master at fishing.

Everyone usually does what everyone else does.

Everyone usually tries to follow everyone else.

Don't be everyone else. You become a master fisherman or master fisherwoman by going to totally calm waters stocked with fish...

It's called Direct Mail.

You Have to Engage People Emotionally

You have to engage people emotionally.

You can logically say, "Your business needs this…" or "This is really important…"

But nobody cares. They care about THEMSELVES.

You have to tie everything into getting through to them emotionally.

You have to realize people are busy.

You have to grab their attention.

You have to offer them something really compelling.

You have to engage with them.

Are you REALLY engaging people emotionally?

Any Problem Can Be Solved by the Right Sales Letter

People underestimate the value of words. They also overlook one of the very best ways to learn marketing: Study Direct Mail.

Today, many internet marketers are very promiscuous. They think in terms of quantity of social media posts, or they push out many, many emails. What happens is they can tend to go very shallow instead of going very deep.

One of my favorite arenas to make money is Direct Mail because there is less noise today in people's mailboxes. Yet, very few young people today understand it or specialize in it. It's like a lost science.

Yet, the key here is understanding what the point of the direct mail piece is…

It's about connecting with people (the right list) and using compelling words crafted into a compelling offer.

One of the greatest advantages you have could be the United States Postal Service. They will deliver the greatest salesperson (a sales letter) to almost anybody's door, and deliver it to them for the cost of a stamp.

It's one of the best things you could ever do to generate business.

Some people will say, "Sure, but I can just send out an email…" Yes, but there are email filters. Just look at your own spam folder. On top of that, you have to compete with all the other unopened emails. Having said that, email marketing is great, but there is SO much of it and it's crowded. This applies to so much digital marketing.

Your chances of selling increase A LOT when you send your prospects and clients a direct mail piece they can hold in their hands, with no other distractions, not looking at a computer or a screen, and they can just read your sales letter. If it has a grabber attached to the top of the letter – like a dollar bill – even better. And you can't do THAT through email.

Marketing is...

What is marketing?

Here are six ways to think about it:

1. Marketing is applied psychology.

2. Marketing is what you say and who you say it to.

3. Marketing is selling in advance.

4. Marketing is storytelling.

5. Marketing is the quickest path to the sale.

6. Marketing is what you do to get someone on the phone or face-to-face with you properly positioned so by the time they are talking to you they are pre-interested, pre-motivated, pre-qualified and pre-disposed to give you money.

If you improved your marketing by five percent in your business, don't you think that would improve every aspect of your life?

People Love to Be Sold

People love to be sold; they hate to be pressured. And when you're a great marketer, you don't have to use high pressure to get people to buy your products and services.

When you're doing a great job of marketing, it doesn't feel like anybody is trying to sell you anything. It feels like someone is trying to SERVE you, not take from you.

Great marketing feels like a partnership.

Marketing gets a bad rap because there are people out there who don't "get" that marketing is applied psychology...

It's helping other people get what they want...

It's WHAT YOU SAY and WHO YOU SAY IT TO...

It's the OFFER and the LIST...

It's the MESSAGE TO MARKET MATCH...

It's all these things and more.

Write an Ad for Everything You're Going to Do

You may have heard of Ted Nicholas, a well-known expert in Direct Response.

Years ago I interviewed him when my monthly interviews were sent out to my clients on cassette tapes. He shared something profound with me. He adopted a strict policy around ideas and implementation in his company. His team could not just bring him ideas. Rather, they had to write an ad and present that to him as the idea.

He did this for two reasons:

1. Putting the idea in the form of an ad took care of one of the most important implementation steps.

2. If the ad could sell Ted, he knew the idea had merit.

This is a mindset.

Write an ad on everything you're going to do or present to the marketplace, and you will improve your marketing. Sometimes the biggest challenge is not the marketing strategy; it's the marketing mindset.

Two Insights That Changed My Life Forever

When I was a dead broke carpet cleaner, two huge insights I realized changed my life forever. They were:

1. Learning Direct Response Marketing

2. Focusing on Continuity

Learning Direct Response marketing changed the game for me. It allowed me to understand the type of marketing that is not only the most effective, but also the most ethical.

To me, Direct Response marketing is time management marketing. It's selling in advance. Selling is what you do when you're on the phone or face-to-face with somebody. Marketing is what you do to properly position that "somebody" in front of you (either on the phone or face-to-face).

Continuity is simply this: It takes just as much time, energy, and money to make a single sale as it does to make a continuity sale. I wish I had learned this much earlier in business. You will put the same amount of effort into making a one-time sale as you will in enrolling the buyer into something that produces recurring revenue.

Automating how often people give you money AND creating a consistent stream of Clients equals a more E.L.F.® – Easy, Lucrative, and Fun business and life.

The World Does Revolve Around You

You may have heard the phrase: "The world doesn't revolve around you."

But, if it doesn't revolve around you, then who does it revolve around?

It's YOUR life. And YOUR world actually DOES revolve around YOU. It does.

Most of the time you are thinking about YOUR life, YOUR family, YOUR desires, YOUR dreams, if YOU got enough sleep, if YOU'RE bored, if YOU'RE hungry...

You're thinking about YOUR life.

To do good marketing, you need to understand your clients' worlds revolve around THEM. They are thinking about THEMSELVES.

It would be great if we lived in a world where you could do good work, and for that, people would show up ready to give you money. But if it was that easy, everybody would be entrepreneurs and business owners - and most people aren't.

To the degree you talk to THEIR desires, THEIR hopes, THEIR fears, THEIR dreams... you will be a more effective marketer.

How to Bake Bread

When you bake bread, you have to use a lot of ingredients - but what makes the bread rise is the yeast.

All ingredients can be important. But, without some ingredients, the recipe doesn't work.

MARKETING and COPY is the yeast that makes your bread rise. And 'bread' is money, income, success, and more.

The #1 reason people have difficulty with marketing isn't because they can't learn or apply it. It is because they underestimate the value of it.

A lot of marketing is disguised under "brand-building." Yet, it is having the right SALES LETTER that can bring you the success you want.

Grabbing Them with Grabbers

When you're crafting your marketing message, you have to stand out. A great way to do this is with GRABBERS.

Grabbers *(also known as lumpy mail)* are a useful way to get your mail opened and your marketing message heard. They also increase the likelihood that people will take action. Grabbers create a unique experience for the recipient and allow you to stand out from your competition.

For example, books can be grabbers. They make your mail lumpy. They get attention. (You can also use grabbers and lumpy mail as gifts.)

But there are SO MANY types of grabbers you can use.

Let me give you some examples:

* **MONEY**: Attach it to the top of a letter that reads:

"Dear Friend, I've attached a crisp $1 bill to the top of this letter because there's something important I need to share with you regarding how you spend your money..."

* **LEIS**: Leis are great grabbers. You can go to a dollar store and buy ten or twenty of them for a buck. They are super light-weight, making them ideal to mail postage-wise. They are also fat and bulky, which gets a lot of attention. If you stick a lei inside a mailing, the letter could start with:

"Dear Friend, I've included a lei with this letter because I want you to celebrate! What you're about to read may be the most important letter you've ever received…"

* **PENS**: Another great grabber. Include a pen with a letter that reads:

"Dear Friend, I've attached a pen to the top of this letter. I've done this because I'm going to ask you to sign your name to make a commitment to something that can change your life…"

* **A PACKET OF ASPIRIN**: Attach it to the top of a letter that reads:

"Dear Friend, I've attached a little packet of aspirin to the top of this letter because what I'm about to share with you could help eliminate some of the biggest headaches in your business right now…"

Bottom line: You can find almost ANYTHING and turn it into a grabber for a direct mail piece.

Start thinking about how YOU can use grabbers in your marketing to grab attention, stand out, and make an even bigger impact.

If You're Waiting to Be Discovered or Hired...

Some musicians, artists, actors, etc. get discovered. They are really lucky to get found by a manager in a lounge, or some other chance meeting or discovery.

But the truth is a lot of successful people make themselves be discovered.

For example, take the singer-songwriter Justin Bieber. He was doing YouTube videos grinding it out. When he started getting a little bit of fanfare, he started going to every radio station and reaching out. If you've ever seen Justin's movie *Never Say Never*, that movie alone made over $70 million.

Some people are waiting to be discovered; Other people realize you make yourself be discovered.

If you are waiting for the *Field of Dreams* and hope that "If You Build It They Will Come" – you will be waiting the rest of your life. There's always a caveat because you could get really lucky. Once in a while someone does get discovered. Once in a while the talent is so amazing, the timing is so perfect, and the thing you are doing or talking about just happens to fit a trend or need...

If the world's supply of toilet paper ran out tomorrow, you wouldn't need to be a great marketer or speaker to unload toilet paper. You would just need a cardboard sign out in your front yard that said, "I got toilet paper; $50 a roll." If you had a garage full of toilet paper and there was no other toilet paper available, you would be sold out in a couple of hours from cars driving by. You wouldn't even need the internet or social media. If you found the cure for cancer tomorrow, you wouldn't need to be a great speaker. The demand would be huge.

But if you are not in a situation where supply and demand are on your side – you better start looking at marketing. You better start thinking about packaging.

If you're waiting for the world to discover you, you will be waiting a long time. You need to make yourself attractive. You've got to make yourself be discovered.

The Truth About Connection

Believability is more important than credibility in the very beginning.

Things that are compelling and believable get people's attention.

Your number one job as a business owner and as a marketer is to build trust and rapport. We live in a world where people want to connect with someone they can believe in. There are so many options and so many choices.

In order to position yourself, you have to develop a level of trust. As my friend Richard Rossi says, the number one question in people's minds is, "Who can I trust?"

Your job is to establish that trust and rapport. No one becomes a great long-term marketer and business owner without learning how to connect with other people on a deep level.

You have to do it through your advertising.

You have to do it through your marketing.

You have to do it through your client services.

You have to do it through your team.

To be connected with others, you have to be connected with yourself.

Making Your Vision Happen = You Need THIS...

Many people come to me with ideas and want to know what I think.

Or, worse, they come to me with ideas and delusions of grandeur...

"It's going to change the world!"

"It's going to impact a billion lives!"

"It's going to be bigger than _____!"

Or, even worse, they come to me with ideas thinking they can abdicate all the activities necessary to make their vision happen without understanding the intricacies of what they want to have happen, happen.

Yeah.

No.

That's not how reality works.

However, there IS a possibility (even probability) it can happen when you put yourself into a group with the sharpest marketers and those individuals doing the most cutting-edge activities. In fact, there's no way to do it without doing this.

People expend more time, energy and money by avoiding doing this, and their vision ends up not having anywhere near the chance of success it could have - if it ever ends up successful at all. It's even sadder to see when not only do they avoid putting themselves in the right group that would help them succeed, but when they think they know better: "Oh, I don't have to do that. I know what to do. I don't need to do that group thing."

You've got to meet and connect with the very best people. You need world class experts. You need to have conversations with the smartest people you can and plan your vision out intelligently.

It takes time.

It takes immersion.

It takes marketing. In fact, it's all a marketing issue. No matter how much money you put into your idea, you have to learn how to set up the model that will make your idea work. There're two things you don't delegate in business unless you want to get screwed: The first is the checkbook. The second is the MARKETING.

It takes access to a Genius Network: A network of people that have unique skills and capabilities that come together and collaborate to make things happen.

Any problem in the world can be solved with the right Genius Network.

Hidden Gold in Your Business

Marketing is leveraging sales.

You can do things with marketing that you could typically only get done by hiring a sales force.

There really is hidden gold in every business if you have, hire or acquire marketing skills.

It's the only mechanism through which you can access certain levels of assets, client bases, and relationships.

You can leverage yourself through marketing.

There's no real one-hour seminar you can give someone on marketing and all of a sudden they'll get it.

I've read over a thousand books and spent a fortune on marketing, and I'm still learning.

Marketing is applied psychology.

The more you learn about it, the more of an unfair advantage you have.

Write Yourself a Swimming Pool

The singer-songwriter Paul McCartney once said, "Somebody said to me, 'But the Beatles were anti-materialistic.' That's a huge myth. John and I literally used to sit down and say, 'Now, let's write a swimming pool.'"

There are a million great marketing strategies you can use to write yourself a swimming pool. Yet, one of the main reasons people don't use them is that they undervalue the importance of marketing because there are so many other business activities that get more attention. But it's MARKETING that makes EVERYTHING else possible.

So many people focus on "image" and "brand" when they are missing substance. If you have great substance, you can build a great image and brand around that. The key thing is the conversation, the communication and being intelligent about all the things that cause people to do business with you. In fact, you should ask the people who do business with you: "Why do you do business with us?" Their answers can become the raw ingredients you utilize to make things even better and more effective.

All of this also ties back to simply telling your story. Think of marketing as storytelling – and you can replicate the storytelling aspects through a sales letter, through a video, through a podcast, etc.

Here's a useful question to ask yourself: If you could only have a five-minute video that would convey in advance what it is you do and why someone should care – what would it say, look like and be?

And here's a useful action step: Create THAT video! (Plus, every one of your salespeople and clients who refer people to you can use this to enhance what they do.)

You can, again, do this through a sales letter or an ad, too. But the point is you want to put yourself in a mindset of creating a letter or video – a communication – that replicates you.

This is the most important thing.

All your entrepreneurial progress requires a communication.

A communication to a marketplace…

A communication to a new person…

A communication to an existing client.

So, write yourself a swimming pool.

How Do You Tell Your Story?

There's an episode of The Genius Network Podcast you can listen to where Cameron Herold (the founder of COO Alliance and a Genius Network member who has built three companies to over $100 million) talks about creating a Vivid Vision.

You can find the episode here: https://geniusnetwork.com/vivid-visions-align-your-world/.

Cameron ended up writing a whole book titled *Vivid Vision: A Remarkable Tool for Aligning Your Business Around a Shared Vision of the Future*.

When it comes to telling their story, I tell people to write a Vivid Vision about their company. The Vivid Vision tells your whole story. Then, if you hire someone, when you're trying to have them understand what your company does and what it's all about, you hand them the Vivid Vision. It becomes a great sales letter, too.

Another easy way to do this is you can record yourself at concert pitch saying what it is you say that causes someone to cut you a check. You record this and have it transcribed. Then, go through the transcription and highlight all the important points.

Trim out all the fat and waste, and just keep the goods. When you make successful sales and record them three or four times, you will have your story documented and recorded.

Before you tell your story, ask yourself: "What do I want people to know about it? What do I want them to feel?"

For example, when I give a speech, I want people to feel inspired, engaged and more capable. I also want them to feel positively disturbed by inaction – because if they don't feel disturbed by inaction, they won't buy. They may be happy and give me applause, but they won't buy.

The cathartic process of having to think through how you will tell your story forces your brain to think about your company in ways you've never thought about it before. Many people try to get creative and fancy, but what you want to focus on is what causes people to buy.

If people are responding to you and giving you money, take your words and turn them into your sales letters, your Vivid Vision, your books, and your story.

Write a Sales Letter

The advice I give to people starting out is this: WRITE A SALES LETTER.

Identify who the list is. The list is more important than anything else.

Products and ideas are not the most important thing. Everybody thinks they have a great thing. The reality is, it's glop. You sell a diet pill? That's glop.

You sell clothes in a clothing business? That's glop.

Everyone thinks their glop is better than everyone else's glop.

The glop is irrelevant until you actually turn it into something that makes sense to someone who can give you money.

Don't get married to what it is you sell.

Get married to who the list is, and how you're going to communicate your solution.

You need to sit down and write a really compelling sales letter.

Use "gun to the head" thinking: Imagine someone is holding a gun to your head, and you have to write a letter somebody will, firstly, read, and secondly, be compelled to take action as a result of...and if they don't, you get your head blown off...

This will put you in a different frame of mind. If you put yourself in that pressure mindset, you won't write something that is garbage.

Most marketing is boring and not compelling.

Since in a lot of people's minds the internet is free, and you can send out an e-mail for free, and you can post a Facebook message for free, and you can put up a podcast for free...people get complacent and lazy about their messaging.

But the important thing here is you need to test your ideas on check writers. (Also slang for modern day versions of people giving you money like credit cards and PayPal, etc.)

Your #1 job starting out? Get checks.

What will get you a check or many checks?

The world has your money. You just need to write a withdrawal slip. And a withdrawal slip is a sales letter.

You need to send a message that will get people to want to give you money in exchange for what you're offering.

So, that's what you do first:

Sit down and write a sales letter.

Then you get that letter into the hands of the people who have the potential to give you money.

If you don't have a system for selling what it is you're selling, you have to realize every consumer has a system for buying...

And it's called price.

Everyone defaults to price if they don't have any other way to make a buying decision.

So you need something to position yourself to sell what it is you sell.

You need a sales letter.

Use Words Effectively

How can you use words in the most effective manner?

You can use words to make people laugh.

You can use words to make people cry.

You can use words to attract or repel people.

The language you use, everything you say and how you say it, can make all the difference in the world.

If you have something you want to sell, knowing HOW to put it in front of an interested buyer is critical.

You want to find someone who is looking for a solution to their problem.

The number one obstacle I see with people is that they undervalue the importance of marketing.

When people have trouble making money, it's often because they have a negative view of marketing.

That it is high-pressure, misleading, and unethical are some misconceptions about marketing (unless people are using marketing in these ways, which I don't recommend you ever do). Every great movement in the world used some kind of persuasion and influence. There was an attraction - good or bad.

If you want to attract more money, more opportunities, and better clients, you have to make yourself more attractive. You have to make yourself more desirable. As David Ogilvy said, "You cannot bore people into buying your product."

The Best Attitude

The best attitude in the world is no better than the worst attitude when it comes to making money.

There is no relationship between being good and getting paid.

I consider myself a caring and conscientious individual... even when I was a stressed out, dead-broke carpet cleaner. It wasn't until I learned to apply Direct Response Marketing that I ever started making any money.

Why?

Because there is a strong connection between being a good marketer and getting paid.

You can be the hardest working, most caring, most amazing person in the world. But if you can't learn how to persuade others to buy what you sell, you'll remain broke.

The #1 job of the entrepreneur is to get paid.

In the very beginning, the thing that will fuel your entrepreneurial vehicle is money. So, you need to go out and get that money. This comes from the ability to influence and sell people, and to be a good marketer (which is storytelling).

If you're more influential, you're going to persuade more people. If you tell a better story, you're going to enroll more people.

Change People with Words

I learned Direct Response Marketing from being in the cleaning and restoration niche. I was a dead broke carpet cleaner living off credit cards and I needed to make my business work. So, I learned Direct Response Marketing...

This led to me understanding how to "Can and Clone" myself. No matter how great of a salesperson you are, you're limited by the clock. BUT... with the right sales letter, you can talk to a thousand, ten thousand, or even a million people at a time.

Back in 1992, I was given my first Gary Halbert Newsletter from a guy who wrote books on how to pick up women. This guy was actually a copywriter and he gave me a newsletter on sales copy. So, my relationship with him was less about how to pick up women and more about how he actually sold what he did.

We'd get into all kinds of business discussions, and that's when I got my first Gary Halbert Newsletter. I then subscribed to the Gary Halbert Newsletter, read it and implemented it. I kept searching for different ways to get an edge, and it never stopped.

Then, in 1993, I met the brilliant marketer Dan Kennedy, and it led to me creating a training course built around my carpet cleaning marketing program. I never learned marketing thinking I would teach it to anyone; I learned it because I needed to pay my bills. As I kept learning about it, I got really interested in it and I thought it was fascinating. There was no internet back then, and I thought it was fascinating that you could send people letters in the mail and they would literally send you money. I was like, "Wow, you can actually change human behavior with words on paper."

I realized there was real power with this...

ENTREPRENEURSHIP

Entrepreneurs are the New Rock Stars

Entrepreneurs are transformers.

They transform bad news into good news.

They take resources from a lower level of productivity to a higher level.

People that aren't entrepreneurial don't know, or haven't figured out, how to do this.

Having ambitions and drives is entrepreneurial. The world advances on the backs of its entrepreneurs.

And capitalism, in its purest form, is collaboration between individuals exchanging money for value.

My perspective: Most entrepreneurs are heroes.

Are You a Dancing Bear?

I have a lot of friends who Roland Frasier refers to as "Dancing Bears." In fact, I've been a Dancing Bear for a large portion of my business career.

When a company is built around the person running it, they are called a Dancing Bear. They are on stage, they are teaching, they are personally selling, and more. If this dancing bear stops dancing, the business stops.

Ask yourself this (especially if you're a speaker, author, publisher or info-marketer):

How do I structure my company so I'm not a Dancing Bear?

An Easy, Lucrative and Fun Business

There are two ways to run any type of business…

First, there's the traditional way, which makes running a business Hard, Annoying, Lame and Frustrating (H.A.L.F.®)

This was the way I was doing it when I first started out.

And if you're constantly struggling to keep your business afloat, then what's the point?

But there's another way to run a business that's what I call Easy, Lucrative and Fun (E.L.F.®).

To many people, an E.L.F.® business is a new concept because everyone thinks running a business must be hard.

I'm here to tell you…

Running an E.L.F.® business comes down to one thing: positioning.

How you position yourself to your clients and customers will determine whether you're running a H.A.L.F.® Business, or an E.L.F.® Business.

The best thing about this is you can have an E.L.F.® business whether you're a mom and pop shop or a big corporation.

It's all about focusing on your customer.

A Philanthropic Organization for Entrepreneurs

Here's a novel concept for a charity that would make a difference in the world:

Imagine a philanthropic foundation for already successful, value-creating entrepreneurs. The organization would go to these entrepreneurs and verify how many people the entrepreneur and their company has employed, how much wealth they've added to the economy, and vet the products and services they offer as valuable. They would help entrepreneurs that genuinely create enormous value for people and the world.

This philanthropic foundation would employ a team of people to help the entrepreneur and tell the entrepreneur to take two weeks off.

They would acknowledge the entrepreneur.

They would send the entrepreneur to a spa.

They would rejuvenate them and totally take care of them.

They would celebrate the fact that the entrepreneur added so much value to the world – and the entrepreneur's company would be run by this team while the entrepreneur took time off.

If you invested $500,000 into an already successful entrepreneur, versus, say, giving the same $500,000 to a start-up entrepreneur, the highly successful entrepreneur would come back and add MILLIONS and MILLIONS of dollars to that $500,000 investment in terms of value creation probably within the first 6 months.

I want to build a better entrepreneur with Genius Network.

They rarely get celebrated.

They rarely get honored.

One of the ways to possibly change this is to have entrepreneurs flip-the-switch on driving themselves so hard, and start acknowledging themselves.

Life Gives to the Giver and Takes from the Taker

I run what are considered the highest-level groups in the world for Industry Transformers called Genius Network and GeniusX. These groups cost $25,000 and $100,000, respectively, a year to be a member. And when someone joins, they will come to between two and four meetings a year.

The smartest entrepreneurs don't actually judge Genius Network based on one meeting.

If a meeting was horrible, we would expect feedback. In fact, we have Genius Network feedback forms to continue encouraging an open line of communication between our members and us. We love to get feedback from members about anything they think we need to know or anything that will make the experience better for all members. Granted, we can't promise we're going to be able to implement the recommendations given; but, at the same time, we encourage feedback constantly.

Genius Network isn't an individualized group where we change the whole course of the group to simply please one person's nuanced desires. And Genius Network isn't for prima donnas - because Genius Network members are NOT divas. They simply want to be helpful.

Also, it's worth noting that Genius Network isn't a company that sells coat hangers or a product that is the same every single time it's produced. We're not serving fast food that will taste the same across a franchise. Every single meeting has different themes and different elements. We do that with the purpose of expanding members' perspectives and building a better entrepreneur.

When a person comes into Genius Network, they need to come into the group with an awareness to be open-minded. If a member thinks something is irrelevant to them, instead of immediately having the attitude of "This doesn't work for me," or "This is not what I'm interested in," a more impactful approach is to ask the question, "How could this apply to me? How could this be useful for me now – and if not now, later?"

What we've found is that when members come into the group with a "beginner's mind," they learn A LOT more. If someone comes into the group as though they are the expert… if they analyze how we run the meeting… if they try to dictate how a meeting ought to be run… if they are constantly thinking how their method is better than ours… this sort of judgmental approach simply doesn't work.

We've found that people who come in expecting to be the expert or guru don't do well in a group like Genius Network.

People who come into the group with the purpose of just trying to use it as a sales pitching platform don't do well either.

However, the people who come in willing to participate, serve, and share their best insights... people who are open-minded, play by pretty cool rules, and possess a "giver" not "taker" mentality, do very well.

Interacting with People

I want Genius Network to be known for the people in the group, not for me. There are so many brilliant individuals willing to share their successes and failures.

I've found the best way to learn is through the experiences of others who are willing to share what they do and how they do it.

Something I learned early on about interacting with people is that you are either:

1. in communication with people,

2. connecting with people, or

3. trying to escape people.

Genius Network is more of a connection group than it is a mastermind. My goal is to build a better entrepreneur.

We brainstorm on a lot of ideas and do a lot of planning, but we focus on building an E.L.F.® (Easy, Lucrative, and Fun) business and life.

Everyone has negative events they have to deal with. The more you can have a group of resourceful people around you, the better.

When you're in Genius Network, you have incredible resources at your fingertips. The question is: do you avail yourself of them?

How to Deepen Your Network

Here's one technique for changing your life and your relationships:

Figure out a way to send 10 handwritten postcards a day, five days a week.

Ask yourself: Who are the clients, friends, and other relationships who you could send a physical card to in the mail?

If all you did was this – even if you only sent ONE card a day – you would develop or deepen your network, and it would change your life.

Have a Discussion

One of my favorite ways to learn is by having discussions.

Almost every problem I've overcome and almost every success I've experienced had one thing in common: a discussion.

It was a discussion I had with myself or with other people.

Many people have unproductive and unpleasant discussions with themselves. By focusing on having productive and useful discussions with others, you will learn how to have better discussions with yourself.

If you have a lot of angst in your life, you have to talk it (and think it) through.

If you're facing what seems like an insurmountable situation, you simply need to know what to do.

This can be done with questions.

This can be done with tools.

This can be done with conversations.

The best thing about being your own boss is you are your own boss.

Nobody tells you what to do. The worst thing about being your own boss is you are your own boss. You have no accountability, no one who will direct you, and sometimes you don't know what you're doing. You have to figure it out on your own. This is the angst of being an entrepreneur that most people don't understand…

There are many entrepreneurs – myself included – that have sat at their desks and were just lost with no idea what to do.

This is why it's great to have a place you can go to and think through things. In the world of addiction and recovery, it's one of the reasons 12-step groups are so valuable.

If you feel hopeless, you want people that believe in you more than you believe in yourself. You want people that are going to give you experience, strength and hope.

This is what the right groups can do. Business or otherwise.

Develop Your Capabilities and Skills

Some entrepreneurs work their butts off and produce nothing.

Some entrepreneurs work one hour a week and become millionaires.

As an entrepreneur, you want to identify an opportunity that is reachable. For many entrepreneurs, the people surrounding them may consider what they deem reachable, impossible. Often times, you have to fight opposition from family members, friends, and the environment, all telling you it can't be done.

Yet, as an entrepreneur, you see the possibility. Then, you develop capabilities and skills necessary to achieve and reach your opportunities.

I was a millionaire by the time I was 30 years old. A few years prior to that I was a dead broke carpet cleaner living off credit cards trying to figure out how to survive. I learned marketing because I needed to eat; I needed to survive. I learned marketing skills, and I applied them.

Develop your capabilities and skills.

If you want a million dollar a year business, you can't do it with $50,000 a year capabilities.

Put Referral Systems in Place

At my carpet cleaning events years ago, I would ask the room full of carpet cleaners:

"How many of you are getting referrals right now?"

The majority of the room would raise their hand.

Then I'd ask:

"How many of you are strategically and systematically putting referral systems in place?"

Hardly anyone would raise their hand.

So, I would teach them that at the end of every carpet cleaning job – when someone is at their highest point of excitement – to get the names and phone numbers of anyone they could follow up with on their behalf. (Today, you would ask for emails too.) I would teach them to offer a free room of carpet cleaning, and for every person that became a client, the referee would get a $10 referral reward. (I would teach them to send five $2 bills.)

And guess what?

It worked like crazy!

The reason is because if people are happy, the time they are most likely to refer is right after they are at their highest state of excitement. In the carpet cleaning example, it's when the carpet is cleaned and freshly groomed. That's the magic moment for someone to make a referral.

The point at which they are happiest is the magic moment.

If you're getting referrals without incentivization and without having a referral system in place, you're just lucky.

Start thinking about how you can strategically put referral systems into your business. Start thinking of when those magic moments happen in YOUR business.

Be A Result Merchant.
Be A Result Generator

Even if you aren't physically selling something or collecting people's credit cards – we are all selling.

We are all trying to sell people on why they should think a certain way, behave a certain way, do a certain thing, or take action on something. Or, we might be trying to repel people in terms of why they shouldn't drink alcohol, or should stop eating sugar, or stop staying up late, and so on.

There are a variety of human conditions we talk about – good or bad – and we either attract people to our message or repel them. How you package yourself and the value you offer is critical.

If, for example, you do speaking, and all you do is think of yourself as a speaker who gets paid to do a keynote, then you are like a high-priced paid-by-the-hour employee.

BUT…if you started thinking of yourself as a result merchant, you could get paid for the result you deliver. What if you got paid that way?

Out of all the people you've dealt with, do you have anyone whose life has been changed as a result of you doing what you do?

Think of everything you offer to people as "glop." Why should someone have YOUR glop in their life…and…how do you package the glop?

What does the business model look like? What does the messaging look like? How do you sell it?

Do people buy the glop from you once…OR…do you establish yourself as a result generator where people will tell other people they really need your glop?

Now, I understand you may not like the word "glop" but hopefully this will keep you from falling in love with something the market has not yet fallen in love with.

Once you package it up in such a valuable way, then you will actually see the value in what you offer and the results you create for others.

Provide Immediate Value

By 1995 I was 26 years old and selling $250,000 a year worth of these marketing programs. I became a millionaire by the time I was 30 years old selling marketing programs to carpet and upholstery cleaners. It transformed thousands of businesses. I've got thousands of cleaning companies all over the world who have built their businesses as a result of my marketing programs (that we still offer)…

I was also Bill Phillips' marketing consultant. Bill Phillips wrote a book called *Body for Life* and was the owner of EAS. I remember meeting Bill at a No B.S., No Holds Barred, Body Building Seminar at the Bally's Hotel in Las Vegas. I walked up to him and I asked, "Do you know Gary Halbert?" And he goes, "Do YOU know Gary Halbert?" And I said, "Yeah." So, he pulls me aside and asks me if I write copy because he was looking for someone to write good copy. He gave me his fax number and I followed up with a fax to him along with my consulting fees, which back then were $3850 a day plus first class travel. There is an amusing story around Bill haggling prices when first hiring me, but I'll save that for another time.

I knew his business inside and out because I was reading his magazine called *Muscle Media*. I still have the faxes because I saved them. Bill ended up overnighting me a check, so I flew out to see him at his headquarters in Golden, Colorado.

Within the first hour of consulting with him I gave him an idea to multi-sequence one of his sales letters that had brought in about two million in revenue when he mailed it to his whole list. By me telling him to mail the same letter two more times to the same list, which he never thought to do, it brought in an additional $4,600,000 in sales. So, I made him several million dollars within the first hour of consulting. As a result, he started paying me $10,000 a day for consulting. But, truthfully, I was actually the most underpaid consultant he'd ever had because what I taught him made him a fortune. (I didn't know how to charge back then. Had I known what I know now, I would have tied it into a percentage increase of revenue.)

Consulting with Bill also led to me learning about how to do contests. Bill was doing physique trans-formation contests, and using much of what I taught him, his company went from making $60 million a year to over $200 million a year in sales in 18 months by using the marketing strategies we created...

IS SELLING EVIL?

Transcript from a
Joe Polish interview

My favorite definition of selling came from my very dear friend Dan Sullivan. He said that selling is getting someone intellectually engaged in a future result that's good for them and getting them to emotionally commit to take action to achieve that result.

So if you just look at that definition, it's profound. Getting someone intellectually engaged in a bigger future that's good for them and getting them to emotionally commit to take action to achieve that result.

Well, if you take out the words "good for them," then selling could be evil. Meaning Martin Luther King got people intellectually engaged in a future result and got them to commit to take action. Mother Theresa did. John F. Kennedy did. So does every salesperson on the planet. Hitler got people intellectually and emotionally engaged in a future result but saying that selling is evil is like saying oxygen is evil.

No organism could survive without oxygen. No business can survive. No country can survive. No economy can survive and be free without sales. Sales is the oxygen that makes all of it work. You eliminate salespeople, you've eliminated the entire sales force. Most people learn what it is they know about cars, about financial instruments, about plumbing, about anything, from salespeople.

It's the sales people that are incentivized to actually sell a product or service because they might actually make some money or commission that are out there educating people about it. Think about all of the things we know in our life that we learned about because we went to a store and someone told us about it.

It's not like you're sitting home watching the documentary on, you know, how a DVD player works. You learn that stuff from salespeople. So not only are salespeople not evil; salespeople are saviors. Marketers are saviors. They are the carriers of messages all over the world. Every significant thing that has ever happened in mankind came because someone was incentivized to sell it.

The problem is the association that people have with selling; they think selling is bad because they say, "Oh, I went to a car lot and someone used manipulation to try to talk me into something I didn't want." People love to be sold. They hate to be pressured. When you're in an environment where someone is educating you and offering you something that you really want, you don't even perceive that as being sold.

That's enjoyable. That's fun. And as a matter of fact, I take this so seriously that everything that comes out of your mouth, my mouth, anyone's mouth is either designed to attract someone to do something you want them to do or repel them, and some sales jobs are repelling.

But anyone who's ever gone to a movie, read a book, gone to a restaurant and ate and then told someone about the book, the restaurant or the movie, and that person actually took their advice and went and did it...they successfully made a sale.

People sell all day long. Where would the jobs be if there was no incentivization for selling and marketing? It'd be a dictatorship. It'd be communism. That's not the world I want to live in. So selling absolutely is not evil.

Can you use techniques and methods to manipulate people? Yes, of course you could. A gun could be used to hunt or self defense or it could be used to kill people or to rob people.

Selling just seems to get a bad rap mostly because of the people that don't know how to do it. People don't realize that everything that exists in the world is something that they'd probably benefit from, from light bulbs to carpets to chairs to cars to music.

ABOUT THE AUTHOR

Joe Polish has an Entrepreneurial Focus on Value Creation, Connection, and Contribution.

His marketing expertise has been utilized to build thousands of businesses and has generated hundreds of millions for his clients, ranging from large corporations to small family-owned businesses. His consulting clients invest $25,000 for a half day of private consulting.

Joe's marketing audio program with Nightingale-Conant, "Piranha Marketing," has continued to be their #1 best-selling marketing program for nearly a decade.

The Genius Network® Interview Series taps into the wisdom of some of the greatest entrepreneurial and marketing minds on the planet. Best-selling authors from Tim Ferriss to Gary Vaynerchuk, marketing pioneers from Joe Sugarman to Gary Halbert to John Carlton, and perhaps the best-known, high-adrenaline entrepreneurs Sir Richard Branson, Daymond John, and Tony Robbins have all been featured.

10X Talk, co-founded with Dan Sullivan, provides listeners multipliers to grow their business and insights for an ever-expanding system of increasing cooperation and creativity among unique ability achievers.

Joe's I Love Marketing® podcast with marketing consultant and productivity expert, Dean Jackson, has become a worldwide phenomenon with I Love Marketing Meetup groups throughout North America, Europe, Asia, and Australia.

Joe's passions today are continuing to develop his Genius Network® (aka 25K Group) and GeniusX. These groups are for high-achieving entrepreneurs providing useful sales and marketing best practices, inspiration, and access to otherwise inaccessible experts and connections simply not available anywhere else.

Joe also prides himself on philanthropic efforts having raised well over three million dollars to date for Virgin Unite to help fund entrepreneurial schools and humanitarian programs.

For requests to speak with Joe, please go to https://joepolish.com/submit-your-proposal/.

OTHER BOOKS
BY JOE POLISH

The Miracle Morning for Addiction Recovery